# The Ink Diver

## Waves of verses

## Ezyln Hanna

BookLeaf Publishing

India | USA | UK

Made with ❤ on the BookLeaf Publishing Platform
www.bookleafpub.in
www.bookleafpub.com

# Dedication

Oh.. To love and to be loved by a writer a poet a singer
or anyone who could tell the world in heart letters about
you

For the ones who kept my heart beating
This is me thanking you...

# Preface

Among oceans of letters, You chose to skim through
these pages whether it is a sudden glance or to keep you
company while you sip lemonade or on a resolution to
read poems this year or even a rhyme for someone.. I
thank you regardless for your time spent here.
You made it here without drowning. The insights I
gained from diving deep into ink are now in your hands.

If you're wondering why I am an Ink Diver of all things,
It is because I find each writing takes me deeper than
where I would like to wander and there are times when I
run out of oxygen aka the hands fail to keep up and we
are back to the mainland, longing for another dive.
It is a struggle between inspiration and the urge to get
back to the shore.

It's a struggle between the desire for inspiration and the
urge to return to safety. The depths of these waters lead
to darker places within us, yet it's a stunning galaxy if
you're brave enough to keep swimming, just like Dory
from Finding Nemo.

I've encountered many exotic creatures that surprised me
—a marine world that left me in awe. Among them are

the Octopus of curiosity, the fun-loving sonnets of dolphins, the attacking shark of rage, the glowing jellyfish that kept me awake all night, the rays of regret buried in the seafloor, and the pufferfish that drew in the sand, yearning for its beloved to glance its way before the currents swept it all away. All of these creatures exist within me, living alongside the undercurrents of my existence. It's quite scary to put them all in an Underwater Exhibition; they're not used to such bright lights. I hope you don't scare them away, whether they belong to you or me.

Each dive brings me closer to the pearls and oysters that my heart has kept hidden among the corals of wonder and unwritten pages. This means the book you hold is a seashell of my echoes. Whether you have a listening ear, a musical ear, or simply a love for the song of the waters, you will find it for yourself.

Let your heart embrace these ripples and find beauty in everything, even in the darkness.

# Acknowledgements

I would like to acknowledge Bookleaf Publications on bringing my first book to life. Without you guys I would be still lost in puddles of thinking of why I cant find my book anywhere at all.

It is only by grace I made it this far...

I couldn't make this happen without my clan...That would mean Papa and his phone call about writers and how you carried way more excitement than I could contain...Ma with her never drying words of support I would never know that secret of yours...Gran who watered my fairytale garden with her own ..Junior who would sit with me to hear the keyboard typing, I have never seen you watch a blank word document this closely before

To late nights with hands matching music tempo and my pals calling me a busy lady..

Yes of course, all my inspirations drawn from people, places and things I have encountered and let them cast stories and random wonder with me pages and yet only the luckiest(didn't y'all wish upon a shooting star) made it here...

and so I thankyou for choosing to stay in my heart.(.I wonder how you all chose a forest ..must be a tree house

or a jungle book fan eh) residential till i made documents
of your stay with my ink.

Verba volant, scripta manent

# 1. The Soul of the World

The Soul of the World is alive
as much as you and me
Hear her breathe, inspire in
the deepest of jungles
a hum of her breath
got in the waterfalls
Lush green flora she grew as her hair
with a new flower for every season.
She paints the skies on a whim
Catches the caterpillar
touches it into a butterfly
Caress the wild as she moves
the fawns she fondly calls
She gives a new song
on every full moon
for the wolf pack to howl.
The wisdom bestowed to fauna
from baby animals to the fiery beasts
The Soul of the World isn't just in the jungle
It throbs and beats inside us all.
In days that we think alike
and speak words unknown
Write things to existence
the touch of creation graceful.

How the world is alive
for it is within us all
even as men turn to dust
The soul lives through it all
A distant memory and a blur dream
Collect over zillions of years
the stars lock the longings.

# 2. World of words

Oh the power of words
like the sky turning black
with a flock of birds
the words spoken at right times
talk in the right mind
To give an understanding
is to have an understanding of words
The words to move rocky mountains
can indeed move frozen hearts of stone
To make the heavens smile upon you
for you mastered the art of words
to make angels sing songs
to comfort unseen wounds
that nobody ever talks of
The potion of words to make
someone smile all day
Words to hug someone from afar
those words to stitch the open wounds
The words to bring dead to life
very words to bring tears of joy
would wipe those tears shed
To be spoken at the chime of clock
when to speak and listen
for two ears make a heart

So shall the words heal through your ears
Oh the words I've wanted to hear for so long..

# 3. The Ink Diver's find

Her dress touch the floor
the floor tiles glaze as she moves
to the sound of air she breathe
the wine that flows in her veins
She catches rhythm,changes pace at moments
when she's sure where her stroke lands
The hair messy from threads in her head
Invisible as she moves past them,with them
twirling over every letter,a full stop hover
but a semicolon to her notes
Wherever she takes step,she leaves a trail in an
unwritten page,
Oh she is lost in the metal case she's dresses
her dress of magic the way it leaves a print
words that would never get erased
the power she holds over
her frock of black and blue
None sees the dark lines,the gaps
amidst words for they are captivated
by her show of colours seen in their soul
Light glitters on her frock
sunrays pause to take her hand as she sits by the
window,
She knows her marks have long sequels

her vial limited like her fellow dancers
Hopes to stay in her white,dusty yellow footpath
A cursive here or two,but with every swirl
like a fish dancing through sea weeds
She sees every word phrase now
skipping with life she gave, the intensity
of emotions mirror in each line
giving her the vigour to dance faster
Out of rhythm lost in her speed
The world turning a blur
All that's left behind is the spinning head
where she roams in free robes tied loose
No chains and no fear but alive
that when her ink fades to just a scratch of pen
She would close her eyes to sleep
knowing everytime the hand held hers
She had danced with the hand held hers
had danced felt fingers tight
as together they brought words alive

The dance of the ink dancer
With every pause splatter clarity than ever before
The one who held the ink dancer
is an artist is what they call
a whirlwind of cavort and alphabets
Alpha for her life ..Omega in her existence
With the ink dancer flying swift

swift like a shooting star untamed
She moves,skips through realms
getting hold of her horses of thought
jotting it as they got her to chase
Her palms held scars and rashes
from glides and new courses she took
sweat merged with ink dancer's coat of paint
revealing silver skin
The days ink dancer got washed in rain of tears
without an umbrella
her stains drenched and puddles made on paper
When it dries each puddle a pond of thoughts
revealed much of a sight
Days when words escape the woven net of word catcher
like a big catch
Somedays on a trance
dancing with a poetess no heed of outside world
for it was her sword to cut open doors
the bullet to pierce stonewalls
a healing soup in bouts of mind sickness
The dancer and white pages the stages
Patient in endless times
listen to unheard tales waiting to be heard
to be send on a quest over any eye that reads
The joyful tears when she reads and looks
at the historic troops she made in books
The days she fell in love with the Pen

so dear giving birth to never lands
How much of a zeal they shared couldn't be compared
No complains as she ripped the white slates
Perfectionist and act
graveyard of paper planes and living words
had her scent and fire she poured over
Oh...the ink dancer a beauty
 seldom be told in mere words.

# 4. The Night Whisper

Have you seen the whisperer
or missed his robe again
as he makes way in haste
no night time missed in waste.

His clad loose as the night sky
dark with strings of clouds passing unnoticed
as he whispers
to the eyes that need rest
A simple whisper and the eyes
close their windowsills
as he sprinkles a touch of fantasy
but were long forgotten dreams of a man's heart.

He strokes the owls as he goes
to which the golden eyes cry 'who'
the replies of the hoot hung in the air
He knocks on tree trunks for bats
to know their time
He looks fondly at a moon
changing her phases
yet her face is all he knows

He shoots a shooting star

and it changed paths
to meet a fervent dreamer
who ignored the whisperer to
close his eyes on the dark beauty

The whisperer's walking stick
draws circles on croplands
a morning awe for waking men

Behold the whisperer
known by the ones
who wait upon his whispers
the ones with a midnight notebook
waiting on his doorsteps
As he whispers tales of wonder
listen well and you won't slumber
The fortunate one be offered
a free ride to many lands
that closes with first ray of morn

The whisperer hums a tune
to the songwriter
who needed one last note
the poets open eyes to surreal lands
the playwright draws the theatre curtain
And the play of the living goes on.

# 5. Dictionary of the Lovers

What one man can conjure
in a simple word
the power it has extended
beyond the letters it was made from

And so a billion poems written
Words more on quotes
and it took a billion more
Many came along down the wheel
the circle of life
finding their own meanings they know of
yet everyone somehow knows

Whenever it's written,
the reader gets to know
Such is the miriad of love
no art,no song,no poem
or no story as in all
can quench the never ending
search of light in love
all of it leading to the light
within one's own
where he shall find the divine

So shall many more be written
be sung,be drawn
and be painted in splashes
and textures ever known
be photographed and knitted
be designed and be danced
be played in melodious wonder
Be lived and choose to believe
Of love and letting many on
the ride of the Lovers
where they shall find
their dictionary of love.

# 6. The Call of the Unseen

I hear a call so daunting
as it calls my name in a distance
Some distance far into a desert
a desert where men die of thirst
I've been told

Somedays it gives an echo
makes me wonder if it's up a mount
A snow capped mountain standing proud
glimmering if purity that none had ever touched

Could it be travelling through caves?
With tunnels that go anywhere
a highway with many routes
reaching the ears that need to hear
As I hear my call so dear
getting closer everyday so near.

Listening close too many walls I bumped
an attempt of my mind
to think of where it comes from
For I do not know how to answer
a call unknown to everyone i know

The same call makes me wag an invisible tail
for it seems so familiar
like a daily postcard in your mail
How does that Call be so for me
knowing just what I need for my tea
the melody that I cannot let it be
as it pulls me up from every pit in a glee

Could it be that everyone hear the sounds too
long they thought was gone and on
like an alarm set for the night
wakes them up in a cold fright

Signboards are just everywhere
Face your fears if you dare
It's a one man path which adds the glare
A path you shall take to find
the mirror for who you are

A believing heart that never tire
Unseen paths give a shot of what is to come
An excitement,a rush of blood
panics may tag in the corner
but the ways of the learner
is as welcoming as life
to not fail to see magic that passes
in the blink of an eye

Oh,I am taking the call to unseen lands
Places nobody has ever been
and see there's nobody to look for
as the one i search for within.

# 7. Hold onto your map

-The Survival Notebook to be alive-

Hold onto your map
never let go even for a nap
for all you ever wanted
is marked on that very map

The map that holds your soul calling
it ain't a piece of paper
or a landmass drawn out of hands
Let it be the map you hold onto
in days of hope and not hope
for it has the touch for you to cope
Never let anyone grasp thy map
and mark wrong destination off your cap

Any mortal born of your land
or that of any distant land
won't have to know or know why and where
for this map you have set out
from the days out of the womb
let not any mouth that doesn't speak
what is to be spoken
shall you succumb

For the joy that shall come
as you walk down the map you hold
is sweeter than any tale ever told
feel the air of purpose in your breath
as you walk down the lines
of a map drawn within your soul.

# 8. The face etched in your heart

Hear ye, oh heart
don't rub off the face
etched on your walls
for they remain
in coldest of winters
the lines that give details
of the eyes that strike through

You shall find the sun and
the warmth you keep longing for
 wouldn't be washed away in rains
that may flood the land
for the rocks that the currents
carry would draw over faded marks

The spring shall bring
two birds from another land
and as they sing their love song
let your heart echo
and the face in it smell of roses
bloomed in the dusk

Even when autumn trees shed leaves

You shall never shed the memories, fear not
for the walls once drawn
of a face shall reside
in its permanent space

Be it twilight or midnight
the darkest of times
might hide the face
from floating eyes

But they shall remain in you
as a mole over your ring finger
a scar that was soothed in love
and no painter
can draw a face as better
as your heart beloved

When the eclipses line
You shall meet the one
who drew on your heart
and you shall know
all the contours of his eyes

The unseen marks on foreheads
occasional dimple that come in sight
the tanned skin you shall see
and look around your heart walls

for they have drawn every change foreseen
**and what remains on the very wall**
**is him alone and no one.**

# 9. The Orchestra

The roosters have lined up with trumpets
morning birds ready to fly
with a slogan of it's a new day,
the owls would stand watching from the tree
tired of the night shifts and neck muscles
the morning dew to wake up the green hands.

The wind would take the bass lead
as it moves through the bamboo trees
the skies are yellow for a wallpaper
The new born daisies sit in their green chairs
to behold the choir of the sunrise

The sun conducts the orchestra as it brings light
to a world in need of the rays
The butterflies fly with forthcoming sun bright
to find another pretty flower to talk to
the bees buzz in harmony,workforce songs

The ants still march for them the nights and days
never count against their legs striking march beats
the shells on the seashore would record
new melody of the ocean mother
as she sings to sea sand and moon floors

The sun meets the moon,gentle embrace
"He'll take over her burdens"horizons know
The gurgle of rivers brushing past rocks
in hurry to join seas blue and dark
The crickets would play their viola legs
a group song do they never call out

The Morning Orchestra doesn't add audience
but whoever listens captivated at dawn
makes a perfect symphony for the rest of
the clock tick rhythms..

# 10. To Lost Thoughts

Beneath the pile of books spiderweb draws
Can it be found between pages dogeared
Did it flew away with the morning pigeon flock,
Is it weeping in lil tweets of the Cuckoo
Does it beat tunes out of old sewing machine?
Will it be found in the old wooden benches sitting for
long,
is it in brush strokes scattered
paint blots like blown sand?

Search for it under scorching sun
grains uncountable and vast,
Did you find it in deep waters
or did you look up ,up to never ending skies
stars stuck on black curtains
Did it sore to the cloud lands in a flying balloon
Is it wandering around lands where you would go

Did it go past astral realms without timelines
with a forbidden lover who ran away
Did it land on the moon and gazing back
Does it lie beneath the rocks of underground caves
forgot to leave a fossil in Dino land
Did the time traveler kidnap it to frozen times

Did it get cold with igloos the penguins made?
Did it survive the Rainforests and journey of the wild
Did it ramble a lot while sitting on a a plane
about the city lights that drew routes
Did it make its way to fairyland and the grooves
of dark horror and agony screeches.

Did it go on a detour to missing roads
Did it sunk with quicksand
Did it march away with troops
Did it reach the depth of Atlantis
explored mountains of Yeti
Does it know the border of land and the sea
Did it jump off a waterfall
Is it with the autumn leaves
or the snow covering trees
a voyage in a pirate ship?

Did it learn to fly with the eagles soaring high
Flutter around with monarch butterflies
Does it skim through the journals and diaries you wrote
under the pale moonlight
Does it dance with the peacocks to welcome the rain
Is it in your bones to get your action set stone
in dreams to take you to better morrow?

Oh tell me beloved where lives your soul?

and the thoughts of it all
Did it get away with papers torn
For all I know is
It kept the pen hovering above paper lands
a wanderer with bags of wondering
pass through doors in and out
in search of what once was lost.

# 11. The Not knowing

See when an artist paints
a picture in mind
somewhere one lost track
hands turn bare human
the moment of wonder begins
a voice or a pull to mix the new
cup of water splashes over canvas
a missed line or an extra dot in the work
what naked eyes cant seem to see
brings what the soul needs to see
nothing that you had in mind
nothing at all..

Beauty of the unknown when it gets known
a grandeur you wouldn't know of
best of brush marks
confused doubtful fingers
is where human turns superhuman
extra touch to the ordinary
comes with a a cost of questioning mind
the instant heart takes on
curious like an explorer in new territory

The same glint you shall see in a writer

a mage of letters one be called
when her pen runs over pages
without her taming horses of the wild
brace herself for bumpy serendipity

What you see with a photographer
gets the time and angle right
a big movie shot of life
every moment a worthy fable
found to those who seek
what led Columbus through the sea

It is what led many to their legacy
go after the unfamiliar
like another day you wake upto
not knowing what is ahead
Only a lantern of hope
lighted with oil of faith
one foot forward.

The unrevealed stands in every dust
loud of surprises, whisper of chance
Face the unknown with everything you know
the word choruses "You never know"
Carrying the quest of the living
to find our voyages never end
Mind conjuring the past and future

while you grip the now
nightmares of thoughts
that arise after the whims.

The Marvel of things not known,
every being holds key
to a secret just for him,
And so it is
The Art of Living.

# 12. The Veil

Time has drawn courage into her skin
woven its intricate needles into her core
even when it hurts to a point of going numb
the lines and swirls drawn add a veil
so beautiful to be never removed
rests underneath the gaps left sparing the velvet skin
holds eyes that have been kept alive
alive in a fountain of hope
how the light kissed darkness
very pupils lets out the starry burn of her soul
sets fire to the torn

The hard coated seeds would grow trees
keep her in such a shade
when flames of the world only bring soot and smoke
dance holding the smoke like an entity
each ghost of smoke round her body
forming halo for the earthly kind
before vanishing to be a part of the veil that glows

Her figure holds wings that only keen can see
wings take far away from home
Home where nobody finds
solace behind walls of pencil

sketches and black Italian fonts change shapes
with the rain of the season
bring forth rainbows to catch
before fading into purple skies

Her nose gets scent of flowers yet to find
breathes life with every touch
mind turns the world spinning
spirals of unconscious waters of intimate self
lips tell tales leave anyone amazed
speaks more than silence
smiling all sudden
What can be behind this all?
Only the Navigator of blue forget me nots
be revealed of true self
where she abides serene.

# 13. Song of the Sea

Every cry of the seagull
Every splash made on the charcoal rock
got beaten by waves a billion times
cries out in silence
the sea sings a distant song
which one may know from the other shore
beckoning sailors to get onboard
in search of mysterious voice for so long

The sea looks raging to unfamiliar foots
but to the ones in awe of its churning
shows love where at bottom time lay frozen
a galaxy left unexplored
whirling in its own current
creatures with torches
haunting bright eyes glitter against flashes
teeth sharp and carved like metal fork edges
swim to the light they give out
following circle of life,moments lived in
utter cold darkness yet they blink and wink

The sea in a gown would have veils that frail down
Each fin moving in it has seen and knows
secrets she hides in her tummy

her hair braided with seaweed entwined with corals
whatever she hides,remains like moonless night
fishes race past before returning to sands
to the centre of Earth where it shall stay
Each newborn angler fish lurching to fight
to tiny cookie cutter sharks
rovering in bluewater caverns
much like us above
trying to make sense of the song of the sea.

# 14. The Wind Prince

Some call him haughty ,Some say he is gentle
gentle to let flowers dance around and at times the
rooftops fly
wherever he goes,his robes trail along an invisible path
nothing in his way remain unbowed
Only the mountains stand still
to his howling dogs

He plays with the clouds gets light to float away
into many lands where the skies need a white coat
There are trees that wait for a ride to sprout
as the seedlings take up high
the aged branches wave them bye

The dandelions and wishes made on eyelashes one day
is flying around my ears in a lullaby
As I prose about him under the shady light
You would all wonder of my very strange sight
for I saw the Prince of Wind riding a chariot restless
he'll play with your hair whether you like it or not
as he takes off without a word or second glance

You would feel the cold You sought on summers long
and when the leaves turn orange ready to color land

He shall have a party of orange yellow leaves
a sore back to the many who sweep
but You must know the breeze brings smile to the one
who weeps

Oh dear reader, What would you think the next time the
wind comes
surely a wave and a knowing he passed you by
He would surely be back before another sigh
Wait let me catch my verses before it flies
 without me completing the lines.

# 15. The Painting

I long for a place I do not know
a place that calls me home
I know in distant memory
like pieces without a puzzle

I have seen it, I've been there
the grasses carry my scent
florets wilt in my wait
the trees with their soft shadows

Tell the moonlight of years that went
As the twilight baths them all
Yet cant find the one to be gently touched
the waterfalls sing of sorrow yet hope
their flowy dresses to which they dance
in their hymns so were they in a trance

The mountains with their tallest stature
asks each other if they spot
The one that longed for her place
Oh the places longed of her
She would know, they sighed

Away from the human sight

there she looked upon a frame
A painting made with magnificient touch
as it spoke to her and her alone

The world and all its living breath
spoke in that one second
She grasped it like a hungry snake
The art only she could touch
a messenger from the dye
as her portrait stood by the view
A million lives flashed
Come back the oil paintings tugged at her sleeves.

# 16. Dancing since

I found a dancer in unlikely of times
A body unshackled of men's logic
graceful as a swan
each step with pride like a peacock
eyes glinting like that of a tiger

The roar of her anklets like a lion
birds must fly through her hair
as she danced with nothing but air
her skin gleamingly fair
had stripes of that of a zebra
yet her movements disguised
among many bushes of the wild
kept her away from anyone's side

She twirled the frocks
like petals of a primrose in bloom
would heal the hearts of the gloom
Only the dancer hears the tone
for the world would play
Whoever listens would pick up pace

In sweat and tears anytime of the day
the feet would move like the waves

like a cat sprinting up in midair
Schools of fishes that swim together
as an orchestra in the waters

The animals embody her
She becomes one with the wild
where her cave days abide
The age when men and fauna were one
comes alive with the dancer of the world
as she waltz like creatures
free of buzzing lands
for she only danced and
held the song hands.

# 17. I belong to the forest

The call of the forest
The greens seeping into your vein
its where your heart lies
in the darkest of rainforests
amidst emerald colors

Camouflaged in the olive greens
The Earth breathing in your soul
for you are a forest child
who didn't know the longing
was for the vines that sprout under
the canopy of trees

The ache to find the sunlight
from the gaps of branches
while the rest be dark and cool
for the magic of the forest to light up

Without maps, to wander
wander the wilderness
the ways turn maddening
But puts the mad at ease

The plants grow towards you

each muttering a word
for you to join them all to find
a sentence for you. Spread over

The heart green aura surrounds you
as it touches everyone you meet
Radiating a pain in the chest
like tears not wept

Listen and you'll remember the birdsongs that you sang
the dances the fairies know
the swim of the bear buried
Exquisite extinct flora and fauna
You have kept, let them not be caged
Set them back in the grass
You'll be one with the Earth
Wildflowers growing wherever you go.

# 18. The fallen feather

Lightly gliding,against the currents
the currents of air invisible
swaying side to side in no hurry
Falling yet so graceful of a fall
lands a feather from a wing of flight

Must have seen the top of the city
must have touched and held a cloud before
must have flew past the pigeons on top of cathedrals
must have been stroked by a loving beak

Must have felt one among many to make a wing
must have huddled in one
against the cold
must have kept the eggs warm
till they hatched to see their sun
must have shielded the babies
from the enemy eyes

Must have thought of landing
on someone wishing a feather
for an angel picked the white feather
let it fall to the welcoming land
smoothly placed on a yellow leaf

Till the one meant to see
comes down the path
without knowing, picks the feather
holds it against the light
as a bird soars past above
the feather so longed
bid bye to the flight.

# 19. My Muse

What are all the artists running around for
never still, always into more
For a muse here and there
they shall find
constant bustle of very minds

A force of inspiration
that comes without telling
leaves the heart swelling
pick the pen, hold the brush
move the earthly body, songs that make you hush
A caress of from an ethereal realm
before it gets to an uncontrolled overwhelm

A muse is worth the find
Muses that come and go
Oh, but the muses that pulls you
to the depths of your own soul
an ocean you didn't find before

The Muse that never knew
He was the poetess muse
An art he didn't know
As he was the art on the go

and the one who found her muse
keeps him as he is

An Art who didn't know of art
but there came a day
when she would know
that she was his musing thought
making him an art
for her to muse amusingly

The time when you read this
You have already been a muse
to many and few you wouldn't know
See a piece of you left in all or in one.

# 20. How a poem is born?

-The living poem--
Out of silence and out of words unsaid
of pain that tear away all comforts
of hurtful stabs and untreated gunshots,
overflows a river of words strewn all over
For it is the portal the heavens opened
a key buried deep in one's heart

Many search for it, an utter folly
when he has it worn around him
like a pearl necklace
Out of sorrows that drowns one in
Out of pure joy no one can contain
Out of hopefulness in hopelessness

The inks call out in siren voices
for then ones left at sea
beyond noises and talking men
for the mind longs to be known
 to be seen
Even when times of fear
as the dark claws choke your voice
with trembling hands shall he
pick up the weapon

Sharpened edges ain't nothing
Compared to the one who opens
himself upon the paper.

Where he shall remove his robes
of robes that the world sees
the robes that hide the true selves
like a forgotten shelf of letters
The robes that cling and rub
against the unstitched wounds
stick to the blood
with sweat of daily life
the pain not taken care of
swells and hums it's screams

The screams left stuck in the throats
Brave and true be the one who takes time
time to uncover his bare self,
his raw emotions suppressed underneath
as it bubbles with the clock of the crowd
ticking too loud and with no bell
but in the one who unwraps the cloth
hears a bell in his soul with a loud gong
for the time has come to see himself
before the mirror in his inner eyes

The river that waits for such a man

has healing touch as it soothes
your burns, your rashes from
the fires you walked in
Oh, it shall embrace you with a long hug
and it dances against your veins
touching your psyche to life
and alive it shall be like never before

And he shall gain courage
to look into someone's eyes
be as true as death and birth
This river of thoughts
thoughts that swirl like a whirlpool
is black to those blind
blind to their degrading self
for the waters pour into all your body
lets out a fragrance where there
was rotten skin once

There would remain a heart of flesh
when before it was rocky mountains
Some dance in those very waters
while others shiver in it's cold
but it shall soon turn to wonder
as they plunge deeper than wells
as is the soul in search

Swim with first clumsy moves
paddle against the changing waters
the very changing waters in colors
from moonlit warm baths
to rainy seasons only clouds

The words with which this river flows
changes faster than a moon phase
and one swim shall never be the same
another for the magic of time and moments
decides its waves

The time to be one with the waters
comes with a cost of such vulnerability
to come into light from black night
from the shadows where he puts false dresses
with a questioning spirit of his true nature
and so my beloved, fear not the waters
fear the fear taking over your own

May you walk over the waters
like no other with faltering steps
yet with a strength like no other
and the naked eyes would see you as the poet
but only you shall know you are the poem
the poem that ebbs in every pen print
and you master waters of words

that fall from heavens like an elixir

Nobody would ever know the thorns
but shall admire the flower thereof
only see the golden touch
not the burning coals
and as you swim my dear
that is how a poem is born
born to tell your name
to last longer than life's little game.

# 21. Moon child

A child closer to the moon
looking up to the sky
praying the night comes soon
Even in the glaring sun lit noon
She would know only of the moon

Freckles like the stars
Some closer made a certain form
eyes held a galaxy
with lure of blackholes
pulled the world in

Find her in black and blue
with grace anyone would loath
thoughts inside moved like planets
She the sun in its midst

An asteroid belt around her
knew the mind defied gravity
daylight looked like vanity
Clouds grey underneath her eyes
a look of being so wise

Every night she would sit by

By the window, you find her by

But she isn't there, her freckles glow

birthmarks reveal a full moon

She was the Child of the moon.

------------------------------------------------------------

This be known of the poet